Friederike Friedel

COOKING FOR DOGS

New Recipes From DOG'S DELI ®

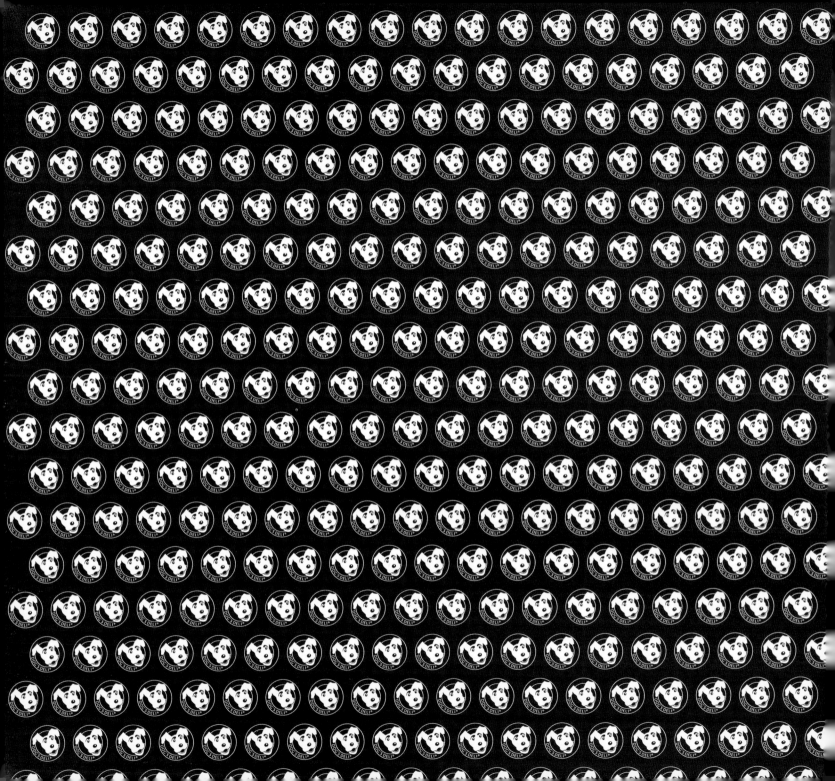

Text: Friederike Friedel
Photos: Thomas Schultze
Design: Claudia Renierkens,
Renierkens kommunikations-design, Cologne
Editor: Vera Brunn
Editorial Office: Petra Hundacker

Translated from German by Dr. Edward Force

Originally published as *Rezepte Für Ein Hundeleben: Neue Köstlich-keiten von DOG'S DELI* by Heel Verlag GmbH.

Neither the publisher nor the author is responsible for any unintended reactions or adverse effects that result from the use of the ingredients. The recipes are not for commercial use.

Other Schiffer Books By The Author:

Baking for Dogs: The Best Recipes from Dog's Deli, 978-0-7643-3248-7, $12.99

Type set in Zurich BT

ISBN: 978-0-7643-3642-3
Printed in China

Schiffer Books are available at special discounts for bulk purchases for sales promotions or premiums. Special editions, including personalized covers, corporate imprints, and excerpts can be created in large quantities for special needs. For more information contact the publisher:

Published by Schiffer Publishing Ltd.
4880 Lower Valley Road
Atglen, PA 19310
Phone: (610) 593-1777; Fax: (610) 593-2002
E-mail: Info@schifferbooks.com

For the largest selection of fine reference books on this and related subjects, please visit our web site at
www.schifferbooks.com
We are always looking for people to write books on new and related subjects. If you have an idea for a book please contact us at the above address.

This book may be purchased from the publisher.
Include $5.00 for shipping.
Please try your bookstore first.
You may write for a free catalog.

Hard Work Rewards

Ingredients:
1 1/3 cups (300g) cooked chicken breast
3/4 cup (200ml) water
1 Tablespoon dried parsley
4 cups (600g) rice flour

Directions:
Puree the chicken breast with water and rice flour.
Bake at 320°F (160°C) for approximately 20 minutes.
Note: Do not place on top of each other when drying.

Heaven and Earth – Underdog

Ingredients:
7 1/4 cups (650g) rye flour
1 1/4 cups (100g) fine oatmeal
1 cup (200g) cooked potatoes
1 1/4 cups (120g) smoked ham
1 apple
1 cup (250ml) water
3 3/8 tablespoons (50ml) sunflower oil

Directions:
Puree the apples, potatoes, oil, and water. Mix with the remaining ingredients.
Roll out thinly and cut out small hearts.
Bake at 320°F (160°C) for approximately 25 minutes.

Contents

Welcome to DOG'S DELI

You are now holding our second book in your hands. Because of this, I am certain that you have also brought a dog into your home and that you are very happy with your decision, just like we are. Billy has been with us for five years and has completely changed our lives. Without him DOG'S DELI would never have existed.

We love dogs, and dogs love DOG'S DELI.

We will reveal a few of our new recipes so that you can spoil your four-legged friend at home. You will see that baking and cooking for dogs is very simple and a lot of fun.

We do not use sugar, flavoring, or preservatives in our bakery. You will find the ingredients for the recipes in your supermarket, and you do not need any professional kitchen appliances. If you would like, try one of the biscuits yourself—they don't taste bad. But maybe they are a little too healthy, judging from many customers' feedback.

The recipes make approximately half a pound of biscuits, or a two-week ration for a midsize dog, like DOG'S DELI's Labrador, Billy. You can also freeze some of the treats and thaw them out little by little. Then you will always have a supply of healthy treats at home.

Don't forget that the biscuits should be something special for your dog. The maximum Billy eats in one day is six pieces. At least we try to stick to that. But when he gives us those puppy dog eyes?

Many customers have told us that they cook for their four-legged friends sometimes. The main reason they often give for cooking for their dog is that their dog has digestive trouble. Or the darling pooch is a true gourmet and despises ready to serve food. Try it once and surprise your dog with a special meal. In each chapter we present you a new recipe to try out. The servings are scaled for a midsize dog like Billy.

We are thrilled that dog owners' awareness for a healthy diet has increased considerably in the last several years. You should certainly ask your veterinarian for advice if you would like to cook for your dog—it is not easy to provide your dog a well-balanced diet.

Like in our first book, *Baking for Dogs*, the Düsseldorf dog obedience school, Knochenarbeit, which means Hard Work, provides advice on activities for your dog. Playing and training are the best opportunities to spoil your dog and form a bond with him or her. Billy loves it when he receives a lot of attention. And the best thing about it is that it's a lot of fun for all of us.

Have a good time baking, cooking, and playing!

**Yours,
Friederike Friedel**

Billy

Billy and DOG'S DELI

Without Billy there would be no DOG'S DELI. That much is certain. Who would have thought that Billy would have had an exciting life as a food taster for dog biscuit bakery? A journalist has even claimed that Billy has the dream job of all dogs in Düsseldorf. Does he know that? I think so.

A bakery only for dog biscuits? What a crazy idea. At first, many thought so, primarily those who didn't own a dog. The first recipes were developed at home in our kitchen in 2005 and under Billy's constant observation. Together we cut fruits and vegetables, cooked meat and fish, mixed, kneaded, cut, and baked dough. Most of the time Billy laid right in front of the oven and never missed out on the first finished biscuits. Naturally, he tried them immediately. If Billy wrinkled his nose or spit out the biscuit, the recipe had to be changed until he happily gobbled it up. Even a Labrador retriever doesn't eat everything—hard to believe.

Since DOG'S DELI's opening in 2006, we have developed over 40 recipes. Banana is the biscuit that our animal clientele loves the most. It's so good that many of our four-legged friends have to share it with their owners. If you would like to try out this favorite biscuit yourself, we will reveal the secret recipe to you now as the first dish of this new book.

Bananas

Ingredients	Directions
1 1/8 cups (100g) rye flour 1 1/8 cups (200g) durum wheat semolina 1/2 cup (50g) ground hazelnuts 1 egg 1 banana Pulp from 1 vanilla bean 3 1/3 tablespoons (50ml) sunflower oil	1 Preheat oven to 320°F (160°C) and cover the baking pan with parchment paper. 2 Measure the rye flour, semolina, and hazelnuts and mix together. 3 Cut open the vanilla bean lengthwise, scrape out the pulp, and add to the flour. 4 Puree the banana, egg, and sunflower oil with an immersion blender. 5 Mix all of the ingredients together with a stand mixer until the dough is smooth. 6 Roll out the dough approximately 1/8 inch thick on a floured work surface and cut out bones.
Utensils	7 Place the biscuit onto the baking pan.
Rolling pin, bone-shaped cookie cutter, immersion blender, stand mixer	8 Bake at 320°F for approximately 20 minutes and let cool for at least one hour.

TIP   Add the water gradually. If the dough becomes too sticky, add some rye flour.

Children   also love this biscuit. Maybe your four-legged friend will share with his small friends?

Made for the first time on:

Billy's Sister
Bubble

Billy's
Mother
Fee

Billy and His Family

Billy was born on August 18, 2004, in Waiblingen as Watermaniacs Beachboy Bill, which is actually his full name. But everyone calls him Billy, Shadow, or Sweetheart.

His mother Fee lives on a flower farm, a beautiful property with greenhouses and endless fields of flowers. A horse, polo pony, donkey, and four adult dogs belong to the family. Oh, I almost forgot the bipeds…

Billy, a left-ear dog, came into world as the fourth of eight puppies. As a genuine Watermaniacs dog, he experienced a lot within his first few weeks of life: swimming training in the pool, cracking walnuts in the meadows, sleeping in the chaos of the flower shop, riding in cars, and playing with many visitors.

His mother Fee nourished him in the first few weeks. Occasionally, however, he was able to enjoy homemade semolina pudding, cottage cheese, and yogurt. He also had a piece of beef rawhide to chew and suck on.

Billy at six weeks

At seven weeks we visited him and his siblings for the first time. What a lively pack of dogs. All of them came stumbling to greet us. Shortly thereafter something more interesting happened. There was one dog that would not leave our side. Later we knew whom—Billy. That was how he got his nickname: Shadow. He followed us practically everywhere, a typical Labrador. He still does the same as an adult dog today.

Once in a while we still visit Billy's first family. And we are certain that he remembers everything because he gets so excited. However, his dog family is probably more exited about our box of biscuits.

If you are invited over to a friend's who also has a dog, bring a bag of your homemade biscuits with you. You can be certain that you will get a lot of adoring looks and make a new friend.

Billy's Behavior Tip
Successful first impression
Teach your dog early on that jumping on people is not allowed. You should not accept such behavior during a visit. The best place to teach this is with the family.

If he tries to jump on you, it is sufficient to turn away from him without saying a word, greeting, or petting him.

When meeting strangers make sure your dog sits and reward him when he behaves and stays during the visit.

Papaya Clusters

Ingredients	Directions
1 1/4 cups (200g) coarse oat meal 1 cup (100g) fine oatmeal Papaya (1/2) 1 cup (250g) cottage cheese 1 egg 3 1/3 tablespoons (50ml) sunflower oil Pulp from 1 vanilla bean	**1** Preheat oven to 350°F (175°C) and cover the baking pan with parchment paper. **2** Measure the oatmeal. **3** Cut open the vanilla bean lengthwise, scrape out the pulp, and add to the oatmeal. **4** Peel the papaya, cut in half, and remove the seeds with a spoon. **5** Cut the flesh of the fruit into small pieces. **6** Add the cottage cheese, egg, and sunflower oil. **7** Mix everything together well with a hand mixer or stand mixer. **8** Form small balls, approximately 3/4 inch in diameter. **9** Place the papaya clusters onto the baking pan. **10** Bake at 350°F for approximately 25 minutes and then let them dry for a couple of hours.

TIP You can also use dried papaya, but make sure they are unsulphured and sugar-free.

Papayas are also very healthy for dogs. They contain enzymes that promote digestion and boost the immune system.

Made for the first time on:

Buttermilk Muffins

Ingredients	Directions
3 1/2 cups (350g) wheat flour 3/8 cup (50g) chopped pine nuts 2 eggs Pulp from 1 vanilla bean 1 cup (250ml) buttermilk 3 1/3 tablespoons (50ml) sunflower oil	**1** Preheat oven to 350°F (175°C) and grease the muffin pan with sunflower oil. **2** Measure the wheat flour. **3** Cut open the vanilla bean lengthwise and scrape out the pulp. **4** Measure the pine nuts and chop with a large knife. **5** Add the chopped pine nuts, eggs, buttermilk, vanilla bean pulp, and sunflower oil to the flour. **6** Mix everything together well and distribute the dough into the muffin pan with a spoon.
Utensils	**7** Bake at 350°F for approximately 20 minutes. Stick a toothpick into a muffin. If a little bit of dough sticks, cook the muffins a few minutes longer.
Muffin pan, large knife	

TIP   The muffins stay fresh for approximately four days. But you can freeze them and have a delicious treat for dogs any time.

Made for the first time on:

Parmesan Crackers

Ingredients	Directions
3 cups (300g) wheat flour	**1** Preheat oven to 300°F (150°C) and cover the baking pan with parchment paper.
1/2 package dry yeast	**2** Measure the wheat flour and add the dry yeast.
5 tablespoons finely grated Parmesan cheese	**3** Chop the basil and add to the flour.
Several basil leaves	**4** Add the finely grated Parmesan cheese, linseed oil, and water.
1 2/3 tablespoons (25ml) linseed oil	**5** Mix everything together with a hand mixer or stand mixer until the dough is smooth.
Approx. 1 cup (250ml) luke-warm water	**6** Roll out the dough approximately 1/4 inch thick on a floured work surface.
Utensils	**7** With a large knife, cut out cubes that are approximately 3/8 inch wide.
Parmesan grater, knife	**8** Place the Parmesan crackers onto the baking pan and bake at 300°F for approximately 20 minutes.

Linseed oil contains Omega-3 fatty acids and is used to treat allergies and skin problems. You can substitute with less expensive oils like olive or sunflower.

Billy always watches intently when we grate Parmesan cheese. Sometimes he is lucky and is allowed to eat a small piece of cheese rind.

Made for the first time on:

Frittata

Ingredients	Directions
3 eggs 1/2 cup (100ml) milk 1 teaspoon sunflower oil	1 Crack the eggs into the small bowl, and milk, and beat with a fork. 2 Heat the sunflower oil in the pan. 3 Pour the mixture into the pan and cook approximately 2 minutes on each side. 4 Take out of the pan and let cool.
Utensils	
Frying pan, small bowl	

TIP   Prepare a frittata for yourself, too. You can season yours with salt and pepper and then eat together with your four-legged friend.

Billy   sometimes enjoys frittata with three cooked potatoes for his main meal of the day.

Made for the first time on:

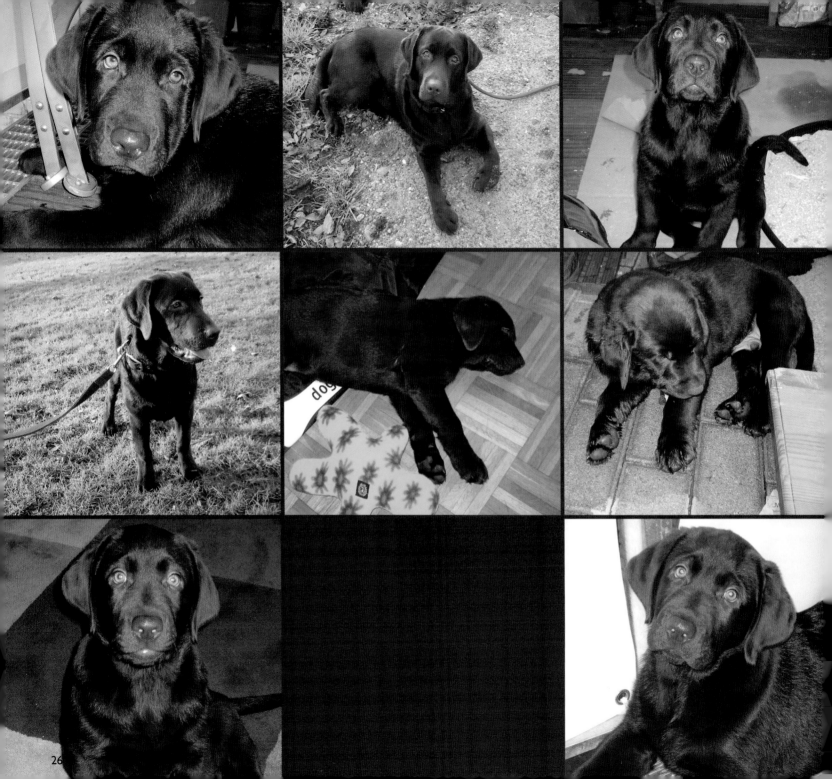

Billy's Puppyhood

It took the power of persuasion, long talks, and, above all, never-ending trips in the car until we knew that Billy could come home with us to Düsseldorf. A serious breeder really looks into who he or she is trusting with the puppies.

We picked Billy up on October 31, 2004.

What an adventure it was to drive over 80 miles per hour from Stuttgart to Düsseldorf with a 25 lb. puppy in the car. As soon as we started driving fast, he would whimper. So we had to drive slowly.

When we arrived in Düsseldorf, he was perky and not one bit shy. As a small ravenous Labrador, Billy chewed on everything and ate a lot of things that weren't meant for him. Even marks on the paving stones were exciting. Once he actually swallowed a bottle cap. Later for dessert he was allowed to eat sauerkraut. The next day I saw a pointy bottle cap wound up in a ball of sauerkraut. Fortunately it did not cause any serious injuries. Sauerkraut is a wonderful trick for doggy emergencies. If something similar should happen to your puppy, it would be best to go to your veterinarian. He or she will provide advice and assistance.

In the first few weeks of your puppy's life only bake dog biscuits that will be easy to digest.

Billy's Behavior Tip

Give it to me!

Practice trading various objects so that your dog will get the idea that he is gaining something instead of losing something when giving up an item. Here's how: play with your dog using a favorite toy. While he's playing with the toy, hold an especially tasty treat directly in front of his nose. When he lets go of his toy to eat the treat, say "Give it to me," or "Drop," and exchange the toy or bone for the treat. Try doing it with various things.

Bon Giorno

Ingredients	Directions
3 cups (300g) wheat flour 1 cup (100g) polenta 1 pear 3 1/2 oz. (50g) arugula 1 2/3 tablespoons (25ml) olive oil Approx. 1 cup (250ml) water	**1** Preheat oven to 320°F (160°C) and cover the baking pan with parchment paper. **2** Wash and chop the pear. **3** Wash the arugula and chop into small pieces. **4** Puree the pear, arugula, olive oil, and water. **5** Measure the wheat flour and polenta. **6** Mix all of the ingredients together with a hand mixer or stand mixer. If the dough is too moist, add flour. **7** Roll the dough out to a thickness of about 3/8 inch on a floured work surface. Cut strips slightly wider than 1/8 inch and then roll the strips up. **8** Place the rolls onto the baking pan. **9** Bake at 320°F for approximately 20 minutes.
Utensils	
Immersion blender, large knife	

Arugula contains vitamin C, calcium, and magnesium and is gladly eaten by dogs.

Made for the first time on:

Fitness Biscuit

Ingredients	Directions
3 cups (300g) wheat flour 1/2 apple 1 3/4 cup (150g) fennel bulb 5/8 cup (150g) low-fat yogurt 1 tablespoon honey 1 teaspoon sesame seeds Approx. 1 cup (200ml) water	**1** Preheat oven to 320°F (160°C) and cover the baking pan with parchment paper. **2** Measure the wheat flour. **3** Clean the fennel, cut into small pieces and boil in water until tender (approximately 10 minutes). Let fennel and broth cool. **4** Cut the apple (with peel) in half and puree with the cooled fennel and broth. **5** Using a hand mixer or stand mixer, mix the yogurt, honey, and sesame with the remaining ingredients to form a smooth dough. You may need to add some flour so that the dough does not stick.
Utensils	**6** Roll the dough out to approximately 1/8 inch thick on a floured work surface and cut out apple shapes with a cookie cutter.
Cooking pot, immersion blender, rolling pin, apple-shaped cookie cutter	**7** Place the biscuits onto the baking pan and bake at 320°F for approximately 20 minutes.

TIP The Fitness Biscuit is only 2.4% fat. If fed in moderation, it is a true light biscuit.

Variety Many dogs find vegetarian biscuits boring. Add a 1/4 lb. of turkey breast to "beef" things up. Like the fennel, cook and puree the turkey beforehand.

Made for the first time on:

Sauerkraut Rolls

Ingredients	Directions
1 1/4 cups (200g) coarse oatmeal 1 cup (100g) fine oatmeal 3/4 cup (100g) canned sauerkraut 2 eggs 3 1/3 tablespoons (50ml) sunflower oil Approx. 3 1/3 tablespoons (50ml) water	**1** Preheat oven to 325°F (170°C) and cover the baking pan with parchment paper. **2** Measure the oatmeal and mix together. **3** Measure the sauerkraut and chop into small pieces with a knife. **4** Add the eggs, sunflower oil, and water to the remaining ingredients. **5** Mix everything together with a hand mixer or stand mixer. **6** Form oval shapes. **7** Place the Sauerkraut Rolls onto the baking pan and bake at 325°F for approximately 20 minutes. **8** Let dry on the pan over night.

TIP   Thoroughly rinse the brine off the sauerkraut with water so that it is milder.

Sauerkraut Rolls   stay good for one week.

Made for the first time on:

Chicken Feast

Ingredients	Directions
1 fresh chicken breast (approx. 1/2 lb.) 2/3 cup (125g) rice 1 medium-sized carrot Approx. 2 cups (500ml) water	1 Cut the chicken breast into small pieces. 2 Wash and slice the carrot. 3 Bring 1 cup of water to a boil and let the chicken and carrot slices simmer for approximately 10 minutes. Let the ingredients cool in the broth. 4 Measure the rice and place on the stove in a pot with 1 cup cold water. Cook at low heat for approximately 15 minutes and drain. 5 Combine the chicken, carrot, and rice with the broth.
Utensils	
2 cooking pots, colander for draining	

Carrots are gladly eaten by every dog because they taste sweet. They contain carotene, which is good for the eyes, fur, and intestines.

Billy often had a raw carrot to nibble on when he was a puppy. It is a good non-fat alternative to beef rawhide.

Made for the first time on:

Swimming in a Bavarian mountain lake is Billy's favorite pastime.

The Wild Months as a Young Dog

The first few months of his life were very exciting for Billy and us: riding in the elevator, running over grating, slaloming on the leash between the booths at the Christmas market, shopping in the store, flirting at the cash register, waiting at the lamppost in front of the bakery, getting vaccinations at the veterinarian, and chasing waves on the Rhine—an exciting life for a young dog.

Considerable effort was put into dog-proofing our house. We used insulating tape to cover all of the electric cables and wires, which made them uninteresting to Billy. Electric currents are dangerous. We sewed a cover to place between the balcony railings so he couldn't get his head stuck. We rolled out rugs on the parquet floor so that he wouldn't slide when he went wild, needlessly straining his joints.

You must get used to a four-legged shadow. We stumbled over Billy numerous times because he always wanted to be with us. Even today he waits next to the bathtub or in front of the bathroom door, and every morning he greets us as though we haven't seen each other in weeks.

It actually took one year until Billy could stay at home alone for the duration of a visit to the movie theater without suffering. When we leave he always gets a special treat. Then the waiting isn't so bad.

Everything is so exciting. A young dog rarely sleeps. Otherwise he could miss out on something.

You can easily bribe a small Labrador with treats to get his attention. This has been a very good tool for training him.

The biscuits we developed at DOG'S DELI are used as rewards at the dog obedience school, Knochenarbeit. The treats are especially small and well suited for dog training with only 1.4% fat. Billy could eat an entire bag with a good conscience.

Tip: Summoning Billy
Coming on Command

Coming on command is difficult for many dogs, but nearly all dogs love hunting and seek-and-find games. Combine both to create a summoning game ideal for conditioning.

Sometime when your dog is off-leash, perhaps out on a walk, initiate an interesting seek-and-find game when your dog needs to be summoned. Place a tasty morsel on the ground close to your feet. Call him and let him search for and eat the treat on your command. Practice this game with increasing levels of difficulty; for example, hide the treat in a nearby tuft of grass.

Heaven and Earth

Ingredients	Directions
3 1/3 cup (300g) rye flour 1 cup (100g) fine oatmeal 1 small apple 1 medium-sized cooked potato 1/4 cup (60g) smoked ham in cubes 1 2/3 tablespoons (25ml) olive oil Approx. 1/2 cup (100ml) warm water	**1** Preheat oven to 325°F (170°C) and cover the baking pan with parchment paper. **2** Measure the rye flour and oatmeal and mix together. **3** Cut the cooked potato and apple into cubes. Using an immersion blender, finely puree with the sunflower oil and water. **4** Mix with the smoked ham and remaining ingredients to form a smooth dough. Add some water if necessary. **5** Roll the dough out to approximately 1/8 inch thick on a floured work surface and cut out hearts with a cookie cutter. **6** Place the biscuits onto a baking pan and bake at 325°F for approximately 20 minutes.
Utensils	
Immersion blender, rolling pin, cookie cutter	

TIP Let the biscuits dry well and store in a tin or ceramic can. They are good for approximately six weeks.

Made for the first time on:

Soy Crunchies

Ingredients	Directions
1 1/8 cups (100g) soybean flour 1/2 lb.(200g) soybean flakes 1/3 cup (50g) soybean seeds 1/4 cup (50g) cottage cheese 1/4 cup (50g) frozen, chopped spinach 1 egg 1 2/3 tablespoons (25ml) olive oil	**1** Preheat oven to 325°F (170°C) and cover the baking pan with parchment paper. **2** Measure and mix together the soybean flour, soybean flakes, soybean seeds, and cottage cheese. **3** Add the thawed spinach. **4** Using a hand mixer or stand mixer, add the sunflower oil and the egg and mix together well. **5** Form small balls with a diameter of approximately 3/8 inch. **6** Place the Soy Crunchies on the baking pan. **7** Bake at 325°F for approximately 25 minutes and let dry for several hours.

TIP   Soybean products can be found in most well-stocked health food store. Only use products that are not genetically modified.

Billy   enjoys the leftover cottage cheese with a teaspoon of honey. Cottage cheese is easy to digest and low in fat.

Made for the first time on:

Hard Work Rewards

Ingredients	Directions
2 2/3 cups (400g) rice flour Approx. 1/4 lb. (100g) chicken breast 1 teaspoon chopped parsley Approx. 1 cup (250ml) water	**1** Preheat oven to 320°F (160°C) and cover the baking pan with parchment paper. **2** Measure the rice flour. **3** Cook the chicken in water and let cool. **4** Using an immersion blender, puree with 1 cup of broth. **5** Mix all of the ingredients together with a hand mixer or a stand mixer to form a smooth dough. **6** Form small nuggets and place on the baking pan. **7** Bake at 320°F for approximately 20 minutes.
Utensils	
Cooking pot, immersion blender	

TIP Let the biscuits dry over night on the pan. They will be good for at least three weeks.

Parsley is a diuretic and can have a laxative effect. It also gets rid of bad breath.

Made for the first time on:

Turkey Feast

Ingredients	Directions
1/3 lb. (150g) turkey escalope 1 2/3 cups (150g) whole grain pasta Approx. 3/4 cup (50g) broccoli 1/2 pear 1 teaspoon olive oil Water	**1** Cut the turkey escalope into strips. Fry in the pan with olive oil. **2** Wash the broccoli, cook in a small pot of boiling water until tender (approximately 10 minutes), drain, and cool. **3** Cut the pear in half and cut into slices. **4** Bring 1 1/2 cups of water to a boil and cook the whole grain pasta al dente according to the instructions on the package. Drain the water. **5** Combine the turkey strips, noodles, pear, and broccoli.
Utensils	
Small frying pan, two cooking pots, colander for draining	

Broccoli   is a vegetable that not all dogs love. A dog can occasionally be fed cooked broccoli only. It is not suitable for puppies because it contains oxalic acid. Alternatively, you could use cooked peas.

Made for the first time on:

Billy is Grown Up

Since his third birthday, Billy has behaved like all adult dogs: Basically, nothing can rouse his attention. He is familiar with many things in his city. Honking cars, joggers, cats, tight elevators, standing in line at the cash register in the store, people pushing and shoving at the market, and small kids that want to become friends with him.

Only one thing excites the normally calm Billy: female dogs. For him they are desirable creatures, but, unfortunately, they're mostly not interested in him. Maybe a present would help—a fact that is well known among bipeds. A freshly made biscuit snatched from the shop window changes everything. The female dog would then be interested in him. Well…in him or the biscuit?

Billy is always the center of attention when photographers visit us. And he loves it. He stands in the center of the action and is eventually allowed to eat a lot of biscuits. Once he was actually allowed to search in the park for Easter egg nests filled with our Easter biscuits and hard-boiled eggs, which he ate shell and all. Who would have thought? Since then we sometimes make him a hard-boiled egg, but he enjoys it only after it has been painstakingly peeled.

Billy's birthday is August 18th. Just like every dog that visits DOG'S DELI, on his birthday, Billy also receives a muffin as a gift. We have never baked a cake for him. He would probably devour it in five minutes, belch, and then look at us questioningly: "What now?" Instead of cakes, we recommend giving attention and time as a gift. Take an especially long and exciting walk, play with him, and spoil him with some of his favorite biscuits. Then you will all share in his great day. You have finally raised your dog to an adult. Celebrate together and bake our birthday muffins for him.

Billy's Training Tip
Spin the Bottle
Drill a hole through the middle of an empty plastic bottle so that you can stick a long stick straight through the bottle. Fill the bottle with small treats. Hold the stick on both ends. Give your dog this great toy and let him find out for himself what he must do to get to the treats inside the bottle.

Birthday Muffins

Ingredients	Directions
1 1/4 cups (150g) wheat flour 1 2/3 cups (150g) rye flour 1 cup (100g) grated Emmenthaler cheese 3 eggs 1 teaspoon baking powder 2/3 cup (150ml) low-fat milk 3 1/3 tablespoons (50ml) sunflower oil	**1** Preheat oven to 350°F (175°C) and lightly coat the muffin pan with sunflower oil. **2** Measure the wheat flour and rye flour and mix with the baking powder. **3** Measure the Emmenthaler cheese. Add the Emmenthaler cheese, eggs, milk, and sunflower oil to the flour. **4** Mix everything together well and distribute the dough into the muffin pan with a spoon. **5** Bake at 350°F for approximately 20 minutes. Stick a toothpick into a muffin. If a little bit of dough sticks, cook the muffins a few minutes longer.
Utensils	
Muffin pan, tablespoon	

TIP   We use mini muffin pans made of silicone. They are easy to clean and do not take up much space in the cabinet.

Muffins   are especially loved by senior dogs because they are soft. It is easier for them to chew if they have lost a few teeth.

Made for the first time on:

Fish Ahoy

Ingredients

2 cups (250g) wheat flour
1 cup (100g) fine oatmeal
1/2 cup (50g) polenta

1/4 lb. (100g) pollock fillet
1 egg

3 1/3 tablespoons (50ml) canola oil
Approx. 1 1/4 cups (300ml) water

Utensils

Rolling pin, fish-shaped cookie cutter, cooking pot, immersion blender

Directions

1 Preheat oven to 300°F (150°C) and cover the baking pan with parchment paper.

2 Measure the wheat flour, oatmeal, and polenta and mix together.

3 Cook the pollock fillet in water for 10 minutes and let cool.

4 Puree the fish with water using an immersion blender.

5 Mix the egg and the canola oil with the remaining ingredients and form a smooth dough. If the dough is too sticky, add a little bit of flour.

6 Roll the dough out to approximately 1/8 inch thick on a floured work surface and cut out fish shapes with a cookie cutter.

7 Place the biscuits onto the baking pan and bake at 300°F for approximately 20 minutes.

TIP   You can use frozen fish. Remove from the freezer a day ahead and let it defrost in the refrigerator.

Billy   loves fish. Some times he's allowed to nibble on the tail of a herring or a mackerel.

Made for the first time on:

Nut Treat

Ingredients	Directions
2 cups (200g) wheat flour 1 cup (100g) polenta 1/2 cup (50g) ground walnuts 1/2 cup (50g) ground hazelnuts 1/2 cup (50g) chopped pistachios 1/2 cup (100g) low-fat yogurt Approx. 1/2 cup (100ml) lukewarm water	**1** Preheat oven to 320°F (160°C) and cover the baking pan with parchment paper. **2** Measure the wheat flour and polenta. **3** Measure the walnuts, hazelnuts, and pistachios. **4** Mix the low-fat yogurt with the other ingredients using a hand mixer or a stand mixer. **6** Gradually add lukewarm water. The dough should not be sticky. Add some flour if necessary. **7** Roll the dough out to approximately 1/8 inch thick on a floured work surface, cut out round biscuits, and place on the baking pan.

Utensils

Rolling pin, round-shaped cookie cutter, knife

8 With a sharp knife, cut a crease into the center of the biscuits so they will be easy to break later.

9 Bake at 320°F for approximately 20 minutes.

TIP You can also cut the Nut Treats into small cubes to make a low-fat training treat.

Made for the first time on:

Beef Feast

Ingredients	Directions
1/2 lb. (200g) beef (bottom round for stews) 2/3 cup (125g) rice Several leaves parsley Approx. 3 1/8 cups (750ml) water	**1** Cut the beef into small pieces and cook in approximately 2 cups of water for about 30 minutes. **2** Let the beef cool in the broth. **3** Wash and chop the parsley and add to the beef. **4** Measure the rice and bring to a boil with 1 cup of cold water. Cook completely at low heat for approximately 15 minutes and drain. **5** Mix the rice with the meat, parsley, and broth.

Utensils	
Two cooking pots, colander for draining, sharp knife	

TIP   Cook three servings and freeze two of them. You will always have a special meal readily available for your four-legged friend.

Made for the first time on:

Life as a Senior Dog

"How old is your dog?" That is one of the many questions that a new customer at DOG'S DELI must answer. And from our experience it is a very important question. Puppies should not eat too much fat, and older dogs often have problems with their teeth. Because of this we normally prepare soft and especially delicious treats for older dogs. A senior dog has already tried many things in his long life and naturally knows exactly what he likes.

Every Saturday DOG'S DELI receives a visit from Paula, a charming and lively 12-year-old female Jack Russell Terrier. Paula, just like Billy, has a job; she guards a lovely stand in the nearby market that sells wooden brushes, utensils, and natural goods. And each Saturday Paula ends a stressful workweek with a visit to DOG'S DELI, just a five-minute walk from her market. Apparently she can find her way to us all by herself. By the way, Paula is an extremely charming lady that stays fit with ball games and long walks. Some times she will bring us a rose or other small present. It is really very thoughtful.

She especially loves a treat we simply call, Delicacy. They are small croissants filled with liverwurst and are always very crunchy. All dogs love liverwurst. We use a liverwurst that is specially made for DOG'S DELI by a Bavarian butcher. It is not seasoned and does not contain any preservatives. But your dog can rest assured—it's very easy to produce your own liverwurst at home. Try it out, and your dog will be thrilled.

Paula's Tip For Fun

Not for water lovers!

Fill a large plastic bowl or basin with water. When your dog is watching, throw in a few tasty treats that he can fish out of the water himself.

Note: In the first few rounds, or for dogs that are afraid of water, try using treats that float on the surface of the water. If the small treats sink, it won't matter to advanced swimmers or true water lovers.

DOG'S DELI Apple Liverwurst

Ingredients	Directions
1/2 lb.(200g) chicken livers 1/8 lb.(50g) bacon 1/2 apple	1 Cut the bacon into thin slices. 2 On low heat, render the bacon in a covered pan until the fat is transparent. 3 Add the chicken livers and cook well for approximately 5 minutes. 4 Place the bacon, chicken liver, and the fat into a small bowl and let cool for 10 minutes. 5 Wash the apple, cut in half, cut into small pieces, and add to the liver. 6 Puree all of the ingredients with an immersion blender, cover with plastic wrap, and let cool in the refrigerator.
Utensils	
Frying pan, immersion blender, cutting board, knife	

Apples   contain pectin, which aids in cleansing the intestines and has an antibacterial effect.

Billy   would prefer to eat the entire serving at once. But the liver wurst is too fatty. It is best to split it into five servings. The liverwurst stays fresh for approximately seven days in the refrigerator.

Made for the first time on:

Crisp Treat

Ingredients	Directions
1 3/4 cups (300g) spelt flour 1/2 package dry yeast 1 teaspoon dried thyme 1 2/3 tablespoons (25ml) sunflower oil Approx. 1 1/4 cups (300ml) lukewarm water	**1** Preheat oven to 320°F (160°C) and cover the baking pan with parchment paper. **2** Measure the spelt flour and mix with the dry yeast. **3** Add the sunflower oil, thyme, and water to the flour. **4** Knead everything together with a hand mixer or a stand mixer to form a smooth dough. **5** Place the dough back into the bowl with some spelt flour, cover with a dishtowel and let sit for 10 minutes. **6** Knead the dough well and roll the dough out to approximately 1/8 inch thick on a floured work surface. **7** Turn the 4-inch bowl upside down and cut out the biscuits. Then use the smaller cookie cutter to cut circles out of the center of the biscuit. **8** Place the biscuits onto the baking pan. Poke with a fork so that small air bubbles do not form in the Crisp Treats when baking. **9** Place the biscuits onto the baking pan and bake at 320°F for approximately 20 minutes.
Utensils	
Bowl with approx. 4 inch diameter, round-shaped cookie cutter, fork	

Spelt   is the original form of wheat and is a good alternative for those allergic to wheat.

Made for the first time on:

Look, Paula

Ingredients	Directions
2 1/3 cups (350g) rye flour 1/4 lb. (100g) turkey escalope 1 egg Several leaves parsley 3 1/3 tablespoons (50ml) sunflower oil Approx. 1/2 cup (100ml) water	**1** Preheat oven to 325°F (170°C) and cover the baking pan with parchment paper. **2** Cook the turkey escalope in water for approximately 15 minutes and let cool. **3** Puree the turkey breast with the broth. **4** Clean and finely chop the parsley. **5** Measure the rye flour, then add the egg and sunflower oil. **6** Mix all of the ingredients together with a hand mixer or stand mixer to form a smooth dough. **7** Roll the dough out to approximately 1/8 inch thick on a floured work surface and cut out the dogs. **8** Place the biscuits onto the baking pan and bake at 325°F for approximately 20 minutes.

Utensils

Cooking pot, immersion blender, dog-shaped cookie cutter

TIP   You could use chicken breast as an alternative.

Made for the first time on:

Salmon Feast

Ingredients	Directions
1/2 lb. (200g) salmon fillet 1/4 lb. (100g) small potatoes 1 small zucchini Approx. 3 2/3 cup (800ml) water	1 Wash the zucchini and cut into small cubes. 2 Place the salmon fillet in 1 1/4 cup of cold water. Cook slowly in the pot at medium heat. After 7 minutes add the zucchini cubes to the salmon and cook for 3 more minutes. Let the salmon and the zucchini cool in the water. 3 Wash the potatoes under running water and bring to a boil in 2 1/8 cups of water. 4 After approximately 15 minutes (test with a fork) drain the potatoes, let cool, and cut in half. 5 Add the potatoes to the salmon and zucchini cubes.
Utensils	
Two small cooking pots, cutting board, sharp knife, colander for draining	

Potatoes should always be cooked before feeding to dogs. Alternatively, offer your dog cooked parsnips.

Billy loves salmon. Salmon is very healthy and low in calories.

Made for the first time on:

Glossary for a Healthy Lifestyle

A   **Alcohol**
Even small amounts can lead to coma or death.

B   **Bathtub Soap Suds**
Billy always tries to drinking from the bathtub, but the soap in the water is not healthy.

Boredom
Boredom only gives Billy dumb ideas: chewing sandals, clearing out the wastebasket, or rummaging through a purse.

C   **Cat Food**
Cat food contains too much protein for dogs. And what dog wants to eat something that cats love?

Chocolate
It contains theobromine, which is poisonous for dogs.

Climbing Steps
During the first twelve months of his life, climbing steps was taboo for Billy because it would have put too much stress on his joints.

Cooked Bones
Cooked bones are as hard as rocks. They can lead to broken teeth, intestinal blockage, and even splintering.

D   **Daffodils**
Like all bulbous plants, including tulips and hyacinths, daffodils are not healthy.

F   **Fat**
Pay attention to your dog's weight. Dogs that are too fat do not live healthfully and do not have as much fun as the slender members of their species.

Fruit Pits
They contain prussic acid, which can be fatal in large amounts.

G   **Gluttony**
Treats are just that, something special that should always be fed in moderation. Would you eat a box of pralines every day?

H   **Hunting Rabbits in the Woods**
Many dogs have been mistakenly dispatched by hunters. Do not let your dog hunt in the woods.

J   **Jogging**
At 85 pounds, jogging is not healthy for Billy's joints. However, swimming is easier on the joints, builds muscle, and is fun.

M   **Macadamia Nuts**
They contain a substance that can have a dangerous effect on the dog's nervous system.

O **Onions**
They can lead to flatulence and are dangerous in large amounts. Feeding your dog garlic, a bulbous plant, is constantly debated. We use it in small doses because it fights against worms and ticks.

P **Paprika**
Green paprika must never be fed to dogs. It is not ripe and contains the poisonous glycoalkaloid solanine.

Peas
Dogs love peas because they are sweet. But they may only eat them cooked. Like all raw legumes, raw peas are poisonous. They are even difficult for humans to digest.

Q **Quality Food**
A diet of top quality food is the best prerequisite for a dog's healthy, long life. Find out detailed information about the ingredients in dog food before you buy it.

Quarantine
Since Billy has been living with us, we have not traveled to distant countries, where he would have to be quarantined. What would we do without him?

R **Raisins**
Raisins can lead to kidney damage.

U **Uncooked Pork**
It can contain various pathogens that can lead to paralysis and failure of the nervous system.

W **Water**
Never give your dog water used to boil potatoes. It contains the poisonous glycoalkaloid solanine.

Y **Yucca**
It is very poisonous and can lead to vomiting and a coma.

Acknowledgments

The DOG'S DELI team would like to thank its customers for daily conversations, intriguing questions and useful advice. Many thanks for your ideas and suggestions for improvements to the recipes and your experience with food varieties.

Each dog has different preferences and needs, very similar to humans. Therefore, the feedback from dog owners is very important to us. This way we get to know our four-legged friends better and can develop new products for them. They are close to our heart.

Notes

Index

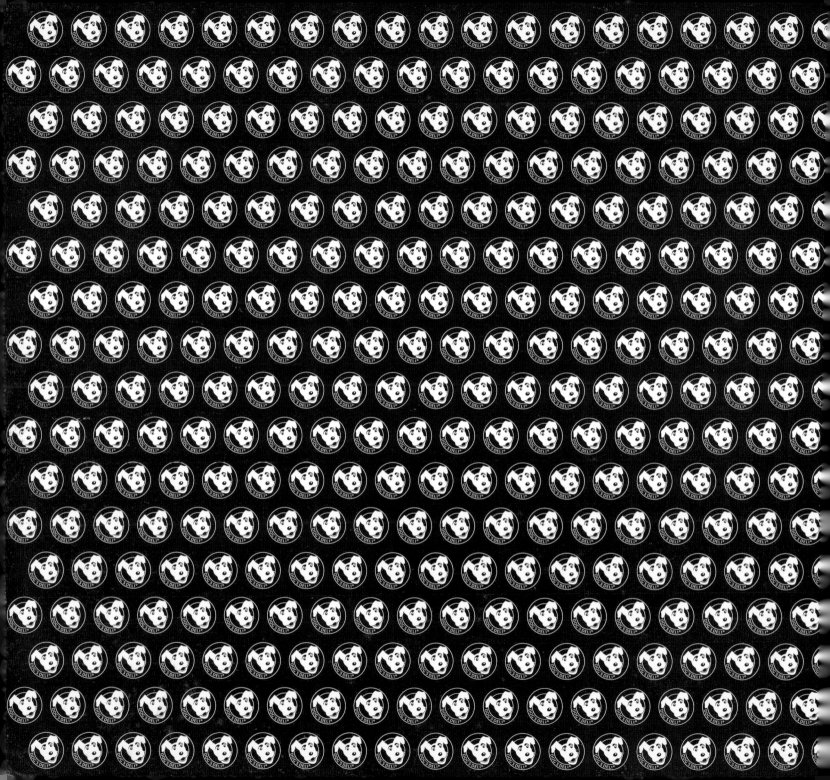